"A great collection of short stories and poems that glorify God within a dad's relationship with his sons. It reflects the influence of a father and coach and the power of sports as they challenge our walk with God."

-Mitch Webster
13-year MLB player; Scout
Los Angeles Dodgers

Thanks for your
years of dedication
to education and
teaching to our
children.
May you be blessed
for it.

# Locker Room Legacies

# Locker Room Legacies

## BY CHUCK PIKE

Tate Publishing & Enterprises

Published by Tate Publishing & Enterprises, LLC
127 E. Trade Center Terrace | Mustang, Oklahoma 73064 USA
1.888.361.9473 | www.tatepublishing.com

Tate Publishing is committed to excellence in the publishing industry. The company reflects the philosophy established by the founders, based on Psalm 68:11,
*"The Lord gave the word and great was the company of those who published it."*

Book design copyright © 2008 by Tate Publishing, LLC. All rights reserved.
*Cover design by Jonathan Lindsay*
*Interior design by Lance Waldrop*

Published in the United States of America

ISBN: 978-1-60604-866-5
1. Sports: Coaching/Basketball
08.08.11

# TABLE OF CONTENTS

# INTRODUCTION

Over seven years ago, I was given the opportunity to do something that every athlete hopes, but seldom gets, to do: return to a sport that has given you so much enjoyment as a high school coach. Coaching is normally and properly reserved for professional teachers and coaches, not lawyers.

However, circumstances arose at Great Bend High School to create an opportunity for me when no one wanted to fill the position of the sophomore or "C" Team men's basketball assistant coach. Head Coach Jeff Langrehr, and Dave Meter, activities director, (whose support, encouragement, and instruction would prove to be invaluable) were willing to take a chance, which allowed me to share some of the finest moments any coach could ask for. Through this opportunity, I have been blessed to come to know many coaches and athletes and it is impossible to name them all. A few, however, have been so instrumental in my training as a coach, I want to list them here: Jeff Langrehr, one of the best teachers of the game of basketball, and those whom I worked with while a member of his staff; Kevin House, Shane Sundahl, Dan Eyestone, John Wetig, Art Baker, Chris Battin, and Josh Lee, whose friendship I will forever treasure; Coach Bo Black and his football coaching staff, Coach Bob Larson, former Garden City Community College football coach, who coached our foster son, Jermaine Barnett, and Craig Fletchall, Barton County Community College men's basketball coach, where my son Jon played.

The biggest thanks goes to my wife Elleen. Without her support I would have been unable to devote the time to coaching; along with my sons Jon and Jeff, and foster son, Jermaine, who understood why Dad wasn't always at every game. God truly blessed me with the perfect family to pursue my dream.

I also want to thank my parents, Bill and Beth Pike, who after many years still show up at game time, the many players I played with and my own coaches who have helped me define the love of the game. Again, while I can't name them all, here are a few. Bob Shanks, my very first basketball coach (6th grade); Frank Geist, who, although he coached only one year at Healy High School, was able to show me how big the basketball world could be; Bin Graefe, former coach at Colby Community College, who gave a small-town player a chance to see a higher level of *the game.*

Special mention must also be made of the athletes of GBHS, past and present, who have throughout this time provided inspiration beyond measure. Also, I want to acknowledge all of the past, present, and future members of the Great Bend Recreation Commission's NBA (Noon Basketball Association) and MBA (Morning Basketball Association) who prove week in and week out that the *love of the game* never grows stale.

Finally, I would like to thank my partners Greg Bauer, Dale Pike, Steve Johnson, and many judges and opposing counsel whose cooperation have allowed me the opportunity to coach.

What follows are some of the words I've been inspired to write down as result of the experiences I have observed and shared.

# FOR THE LOVE OF THE GAME

"For the Love of the Game" is perhaps the best example of what sports can teach in the most disappointing of circumstances. When I first started to coach, one of the things I struggled with the most was a season that ended before its full potential was realized. I was an assistant on several basketball teams during this time where we thought we would achieve great things, but still fell short. There were also several football and track teams of which Jermaine was a part that failed to reach all of their goals. Although I was able to see how the professional coaches worked through it and came to understand their philosophies, it all came to a head in November of 2003. The 2003 GBHS football team was one of the best ever and seemed destined for a state championship. However, that night in Salina, after a tremendous effort, the season ended. After a game that included points being erased from the board, the pain everyone felt was immense. They were a special group, and I felt some affinity not only because I had coached some of them, but also because the senior classmen were freshmen when I first started and we had "grown up" together. Unlike some of the others, this poem exactly describes an event. I slept poorly and woke up early, before light. It was then, as I pondered how this could have happened to a team who wanted it so much, that I heard His voice command me to write down these words. The pain still comes, but I understand now how the coaches I admire return season after season with a fresh attitude and a new set of goals.

> But lay up for yourselves treasures in heaven, where neither moth nor rust doth corrupt, and where thieves do not break through nor steal: For where your treasure is, there will your heart be also.
>
> Mathew 6:20–21 (KJV)

# For The Love Of The Game

In the dark before dawn, on the morning after,
The night that ended our joy and our laughter.
I wake up with the pain and hear myself say
Why do we coach, and why do we play?
And the Lord answers back, quickly to me,
You should know the answer, it's plain to see,
For courage, discipline and lessons of life,
We will endure all the pain and the strife.
To strengthen our bodies and minds as well,
Is reason enough to answer each bell.
For the chance to compete for the number one prize,
We choose to risk a few tears in our eyes.
But above all else, there is one final claim,
We do it all for the love of the game.
11/8/2003

# HOLD THE ROPE

"Hold the Rope" was also born from football, although its message is one for all sports and life as well. During the summer, Coach Bo Black had sent out his traditional letter to his team in preparation for the fall campaign. Jon was a part of that team, so he shared the letter with me. I liked the message, but didn't think too much of it until we went to watch Jermaine's GCCC team take on Coffeyville. Although GCCC had a team worthy of many opponents, they fell that night. Coach Bob Larson's public post-game speeches, win or lose, were legendary, and this night was no exception. He gave a passionate speech on "holding the rope," and how they had let go. On the long drive back to Great Bend, the words came to me, with the usual instruction to write them down. I believe the message is one of life, as well as sports, and I thank both coaches for their inspiration.

> Greater love hath no man than this, that a man lay down his life for his friends.
>
> John 15:13 (KJV)

# Hold The Rope

The call went out to the rescue team,
A soul was lost, or so it would seem.
The night was dark and the cliff was steep,
But they had their duty and an oath to keep.
Their leader knew he would descend the slope,
But the question remained, "Who would hold the rope?"
Two of the men were strong and stout,
So his choice of the third left some room for doubt.
For this man was small, and his build was slight,
Yet hold it he did, though the rope did bite.
Just how did he know, we all may ask,
That the man he chose was up for the task.
It wasn't an issue of strength or size,
But what he saw when he looked in his eyes.
So when it's your turn to hold the rope,
Never despair, and never lose hope.
For it's not the strength in your hands or your head,
That lets you hold on, when the blood runs red.
But the faith in your heart and the love for your friend,
That makes you hold on to the very end.

9/5/2004

# ANSWER THE CALL

"Answer the Call" was my first attempt to write a message to Jon and his fellow teammates, many of whom I had worked with since first grade, about making the most of their opportunities. If there is a common theme among former players, particularly old men, it is about what could have been, or "I wish I knew then what I know now." While I may not always be successful, this is a message I want all athletes to understand. I had intended this to be a theme for the basketball team Jon's junior year, but as you will see next, God had other plans.

> So the last shall be first, and the first last: for many be called, but few chosen.
>
> Matthew 20:16 (KJV)

## Answer The Call

When it's third and long and the wind's in your face
One lap to go and you're out of first place,
The throw's to first, and you're caught off the bag,
You feel the weight and your shoulders sag.
What happens next is never quite clear,
But here is a way to master the fear.
For in each of us God has placed a voice,
Heed it or not, is always the choice.
Wins and losses are but means to an end,
As how we finish, is the goal we tend.
So with the clock winding down, call for the ball
Leave no room for doubt, give it your all.
Then later in life, when the wolf's at your door
Smile and know you've been there before.
Trophies and honors are fine to achieve
But the greatest reward is the heart to believe.
Many suit up, and quite a few fall,
But those who prevail, learn to answer the call.

10/1/2004

# FULFILL THE DREAM

"Fulfill the Dream" was another message given to me for Jon and his teammates, but it was specific. Ever since he was small, we had always prepared to contend for a state championship. We made every appearance by Great Bend at the state tournament, and even went some years when Great Bend did not qualify, just so that we would know what it was like. While I was hopeful, even though we were coming off of a poor season the previous year, I did not know when I wrote down these words in October that this team would fully embrace the philosophies of Coach Langrehr and our coaching staff, and carry the tradition of GBHS basketball to new heights.

> The prophet that hath a dream, let him tell a dream; and he that hath my word, let him speak my word faithfully. What [is] the chaff to the wheat? saith the LORD.
>
> Jeremiah 23:28 (KJV)

# Fulfill the Dream

From the day you picked up your very first ball
And took aim at the goal that seemed so tall,
The seed was planted, a desire laid
It began to grow with the first game you played.
Those early games when you struggled to score
Weren't always pretty, but they opened the door.
So you dribbled and shot, practiced and ran
Each game that you played was just part of the plan.
You've been coached and taught the tools of the trade
And the years reflect the progress you made.
You know you're ready, the picture is clear
The time is now and the place is here.
Be one in your purpose, be one as a team
Go out together and fulfill the dream.

10/16/2004

# TEAM

The season had progressed and many records were set, including a lengthy win streak, undefeated at home, and a share of the conference championship. But with two painful losses to end the season, the future was anything but certain. However, the team concept took over. First, the seniors had a closed-door meeting. Second, Coach Wetig and Coach Baker refined the theme of "Right Here, Right Now," which along with Coach Langrehr's, "It's not who we play, it's how," were embraced by the team. Each accepted his role. Finally, Bill Cordes, an outstanding motivational speaker, volunteered to speak to our team, as his stepdaughter was one of our managers. He gave a presentation on the importance of trust that crystallized in my mind, and I think in the heart of every one present, that a foundation of trust is the key to any successful joint venture, a concept that is true in sports as well as life. As you will see later, it is a concept that would be reinforced in the months and years to come. It was his first presentation to our team, but it would not be his last as he spoke to our team at critical times over the next two years. I don't want to give away his trade secrets, but if you have the chance to hear him, I strongly recommend that you do so. In a lifetime of sports with many memorable moments, he has supplied some of my favorite memories. We won our first round of sub-state, and were set to face a major rival, Hays at Liberal. "TEAM" was written on the bus ride down, and reflects the importance of the concept. In a spirited game, we moved one step closer to fulfilling the dream, advancing to state.

> That there should be no schism in the body; but [that] the members should have the same care one for another. And whether one member suffer, all the members suffer with it; or one member be honoured, all the members rejoice with it.
>
> I Corinthians 12:25–26 (KJV)

## Team

"T" is for *trust*
With which we begin.
"E" is for the *effort*
Which it takes to win.
*"A"* brings *attitude*
To meet the test.
"M" marks our *mission*
To be the best.
The four join together
A force to make.
To face any challenge,
The prize to take.
3/5/2005

# WHAT YOU WILL DO

During what still sometimes seems like a dream, GBHS defeated their first two opponents at the state tournament in Topeka. As in the sub-state games, each player accepted their role and gave maximum effort in the victories. This earned the chance to face top-seeded Topeka West in the championship game. A talented and physical team, not many outside of the GBHS faithful gave GBHS much chance. After a long night of watching tape and discussing various strategies, Coach Langrehr determined that we would play our game and not change what had brought the team to this point, giving action to the words "It's not who but how." Once again, coupled with the urgency of "Right Here and Right Now," the team and staff prepared for the big game. "What you will do" was penned in a practice gym and posted before the game as a statement of confidence in what this team had already shown. It proved to be prophetic in nature, as the Panthers took down Topeka West to garner the school's first men's state basketball championship.

> Know ye not that they which run in a race run all, but one receiveth the prize? So run, that ye may obtain.
>
> I Corinthians 9:24 (KJV)

## What You Will Do

What will you do
When its 1 vs. 2?
How will you play
When you play the big game?
So many questions,
Yet the answer's the same.
You will trust in your team,
They won't let you fall.
You will hold nothing back,
You will give it your all.
When there's nothing left,
And you lie on the floor,
You won't have to worry,
About the final score.
3/12/2005

# THE DREAM FULFILLED

After we won, in preparation for the team banquet, it was suggested that I needed to write another poem of a dream fulfilled. Particularly for our seniors, but also for the rest of the team, I wanted something to carry with them beyond high school. After meditating, "The Dream Fulfilled" was written as a message for their future as I look forward to seeing the young men they have and will become.

> Thus saith the LORD, Let not the wise [man] glory in his wisdom, neither let the mighty [man] glory in his might, let not the rich [man] glory in his riches: But let him that glorieth glory in this, that he understandeth and knoweth me, that I [am] the LORD which exercise loving kindness, judgment, and righteousness, in the earth: for in these [things] I delight, saith the LORD."
>
> Jeremiah 9:23–24 (KJV)

chuck pike

## The Dream Fulfilled

You had the dream.
You built a team.
You got it done.
Now the trophy's won.
But this you must know
There's new seeds to sow.
More games to play,
A dream for each day.
For each dream that's complete
Birth's a new goal to meet.
So always remember
And keep in your heart,
How this dream was fulfilled
As new dreams you start.

3/17/2005

# STEP UP TO THE PLATE

The baseball season following our state championship was also highly anticipated. Several members of our basketball team were on the baseball team, and many of the others were good friends. In an attempt to keep things going, "Step up to the Plate" was written. Highly ranked all year, this team also adopted the concepts that make for great teams, and stand as an example to future athletes. Although they were upset in the regional finals, if baseball regionals were a series, I think they would have proven to be champions. This is the only purely baseball poem I have been inspired to write, but with our son, Jeff, pursuing baseball, I should probably add "to this point in time" to those words. I hope when he gets his chance he will "Step up to the Plate."

> And Caleb stilled the people before Moses, and said, "Let us go up at once, and possess it; for we are well able to overcome it."
>
> Numbers13:30 (KJV)

## Step Up to the Plate

It's a different season, a different game
But the truths you've learned are ever the same.
So as you hit and run, catch and throw
Plant the seeds and watch them grow.
It begins with trust, in yourself, your team,
You need a vision, a plan, a scheme.
Honor your Maker with strength and skill
Forge with your teammates a single will.
Accept your position, embrace your role
Lay down yourself to reach the goal.
Own your errors, but play it smart
Keep your focus, never lose heart.
In every game, in every inning
See each pitch as a new beginning.
Give all that you have, more if you dare
The rewards you'll reap are beyond compare.
Trophies tarnish and cheers will fade
But you will remember just how you played.
Now is the time, you don't want to wait
For it's your turn, step up to the plate.

4/12/2005

# KEEP THE TRUST

"Keep the Trust" was written in advance of our summer camp prior to the start of Jon's senior year. I wanted a message of the need to continue what had been learned and further develop the importance of trust. In the back of my mind, I thought this might be our new theme for the upcoming season. Again, I was wrong because the best was yet to come.

> Some [trust] in chariots, and some in horses: but we will remember the name of the LORD our God.
>
> Psalms 20:7 (KJV)

## Keep the Trust

It was placed in you when you first took the floor,
With each year you played, it's grown ever more
You've accomplished much with hard work and sweat,
But you know in your heart you're not done yet.
For what burns inside, shines in your eyes
As it drives your quest for another prize.
Forever a part of a champion team,
You know the power of a common dream.
Now it's your turn, and now its your time,
Prepare yourself for another climb.
Honor those who marked the way,
And for this time, give thanks each day.
Resist the lure of your own fame,
Lose yourself in the love of the game.
For far too soon the last horn will sound,
The trophy awarded, a champion crowned
Do all you can, do all that you must,
To make your mark and thus keep the *trust*.
6/23/2005

# DARE TO BELIEVE

Jon's senior year started with football, and Coach Bo Black is one of the great masters of motivation. I have learned a great deal from him, both as a coach and as a parent of children who play a sport. He has always challenged his players to "Dare to Be Great." I have always wanted to try to build on that concept, along with other parts of his philosophy. "Dare to Believe" was my humble attempt to contribute to his football program. Based upon my observations, he has created not just good teams but good young men. Sometimes, in life, we must all "Dare to Believe."

> Jesus said unto him, "If thou canst believe, all things [are] possible to him that believeth."
>
> Mark 9:23 (KJV)

## Dare to Believe

Stand in the tunnel with your brothers, your team
And heed these words, then live the dream.
Thank your Maker for the chance to play
His Spirit must guide your steps each day.
Honor those whose names line your wall
Hear your coaches as your name they call.
See each play as your moment in time
Never look back as each hill you climb.
Keep one hand free to help your friend
Love each other 'till the very end.
This is your mission, this is your quest
Give all you have, no less than your best.
For the goals you set for this band to achieve
Are there to be seized if you *dare to believe.*
7/29/2005

# GET IN

Having been around sports in some form for over thirty-five years, it is always a treat to hear something you haven't heard before. Coach Black assigns each of his assistants a week of motivation. One of his assistants (I think it was Coach Vesta) brought the illustration of a famous NFL coach and his wheelbarrow. I had never heard this illustration before and it fascinated me, not only because of its athletic implications but the spiritual and life applications as well. Once again, after meditating while driving, which is often where these poems are written, the story was put to rhyme.

> But wilt thou know, O vain man, that faith without works is dead?
>
> James 2:20 (KJV)

## Get In

It caused a stir, when he came to town
As he pushed his wheelbarrow, up and down.
For he made a boast, he said he would keep,
To push it across, the chasm so deep.
"I'll walk the tightrope, for I know how"
He said to all, then left with a bow.
Most of them laughed and called him a loon,
But one of the men heard a different tune.
So he secretly watched, the man unafraid,
While he practiced, wobbled and swayed.
And as he watched, his skill did grow,
So the man saw the chance, his friends to show.
So he bet them that, he'd go all the way,
While he waited, for that fateful day.
They all were there, at the top of the hill
" You'll do it" he cheered," I know you will!"
The man at the wire, stopped and turned
His face was as stone, and his eyes they burned.
"If you believe, I can do what I say,

Don't sit on the sideline, come on, let's play.
If you know, that you're going to win,
Give someone your money, come on, get in."
The truth is simple, and plain as can be,
Words are fine, but real faith is the key.
So don't hold back, dive in with both feet,
You'll find your goals, you're prepared to meet.
9/14/2005

# THE LOSS

We've all heard the various statements made after a loss. *Maybe we needed it. Learn from it,* etc. From painful experience, I don't think there's ever an easy answer. In an early season loss to a very good Blue Valley team, GBHS football played one of their very best games, but still lost. Once again, after meditating on what this meant, I was given the words to "The Loss." I don't think it has made it any easier, but it has at least a therapeutic effect for me, and when they occur, I have dusted it off to remind me that it is just one game—one moment in a lifetime.

> I returned, and saw under the sun, that the race [is] not to the swift, nor the battle to the strong, neither yet bread to the wise, nor yet riches to men of understanding, nor yet favour to men of skill; but time and chance happeneth to them all.
>
> Ecclesiastes 9:11 (KJV)

## The Loss

The cards are dealt, the hand is played.
For a loss, a price is paid
It's never wanted, never needed,
But its lessons must be heeded.
Its effect is never certain,
A single scene? Or final curtain?
Stand as one? Or fall apart?
It's all a matter of the heart.
A lone uninvited guest
Must not spoil all the rest
The pain will ease, the wounds will heal
But only if your faith is real
Practice harder, prepare longer,
As your bond grows ever stronger.
Look within and count the cost
And you will find all that was lost.
9/17/2005

# FULFILL THE DREAM II

After the success of last season's "Fulfill the Dream," it seemed unlikely that I would be able to duplicate the message I wanted to give to Jon and the rest of his team for his senior year. I couldn't do it, but I was given the words to "Fulfill the Dream II." Credit for the secondary title ("New Team, Same Dream, New Season, Same Reason") goes to Jeff Pike, as he gave me the idea. The rest was drawn from what we had learned together last season. Once again, I did not fully realize how prophetic in nature it would prove to be, as this team would prove to be one of the best ever. It also started my most prolific inspiration to write. Was it because it was Jon's senior year, or was it the people I was around who inspired me? Probably more than a little of each.

> For a dream cometh through the multitude of business; and a fool's voice [is known] by multitude of words.
>
> Ecclesiastes 5:3 (KJV)

# Fulfill The Dream II:
*(New Team, Same Dream, New Season, Same Reason)*

Put up your ring, and lace up your shoes,
As great as it was, it's yesterday's news.
For now it is time to renew the dream.
Let faith be your guide as you build your team.
Make the most of each touch, each practice, each game
For the reason you play is always the same.
Your love for the game has brought you this far,
You've honed your skills, you've raised the bar.
With trust as your pledge, your motto, your creed,
Let the team grow strong as they follow your lead.
Give more than you have, be more than you are,
Endeavor to make each teammate a star.
Now is the time, yes, here is the place,
Strengthen each other for the challenge you face.
You've trained for this moment, trained for this day,
So give your best each step of the way.
No goal is too great, no mark too high,
For the team that believes, and understands why.

10/22/2005

# GAME TIME

As the season began, we practiced really hard. Even though we had lost what appeared to be some key players, there was a great deal of anticipation as the season started. In addition to our other motivational sayings, Coach Langrehr had presented "Never Underestimate the Heart of a Champion," a theme we would carry all season, along with the others. "Game Time" was written to convey the importance of the first game. The team not only won the first game, but won the Hays City Shootout, the seasoning opening tournament. They went on to win two more games before the Christmas break.

> But let every man prove his own work, and then shall he have rejoicing in himself alone, and not in another.
>
> Galatians 6:4 (KJV)

## Game Time

You've practiced long
You've practiced hard.
With your teammates
You have sparred.
You've honed your skills,
Sharpened your mind.
And with each day
More strength you find
You've seen your foe
You know your team.
Yes this is real
Though like a dream.
You've heard your coach
You've read these lines.
Your spirit rises
You know the signs
Let nothing take
From you this day
The joy you find

In this game you play,
*For its game time!*
11/30/2005

# DON'T REST

"Don't Rest" was a message to the team encouraging them to get better during the long Christmas Break, and to reinforce the lessons they had learned. By now it was clear that they could become a very good team, but they would need to continue working hard.

> And let us not be weary in well doing: for in due season we shall reap, if we faint not.
>
> Galatians 6:9 (KJV)

## Don't Rest

You look at your record
And you're 5 and "O"
A very good start
But there's a long way to go.
You've put up the points
And played some "D"
But you're not yet as good
As you know you can be.
You must work ever harder
And with every day test
The effort you give
To be your best.
Your opponents will seek
To turn up the heat
Renew your *team's trust*
Each challenge to meet.
For the champion's heart
Which beats in your chest
Will take you there
If your *game* doesn't rest.
12/11/2005

# DON'T LOOK DOWN

"Don't Look Down" came to me as I was driving on the day ahead of our game at Hays following the Christmas break. Perhaps it was too obscure, or maybe I missed the boat, but I wanted them to focus on what was to be done, not what they had done. In any event, we lost a closely contested game that gave me the opportunity to not only consider "The Loss," but gave rise to what I think is a much better follow-up poem.

> And Jesus said unto him, "No man, having put his hand to the plough, and looking back, is fit for the kingdom of God."
>
> Luke 9:62 (KJV)

# Don't Look Down

Climbers well, these proverbs know
It's not how high, but what's left to go.
Trust your team to hold your rope
And you'll ascend the steepest slope.
To reach the peak, your goal is clear
Respect the rock, discard all fear.
For in each season, game, or day
Mountains appear to stand in your way.
Prepare yourself as you start to climb
Conquer each one a step at a time.
Focus on, the trophy, the crown,
Never lose heart, and *never look down!*
1/10/2006

# NO EXCUSES

After the loss at Hays, as a staff we tried to analyze where we had gone wrong in our preparation, strategy, etc. While there were a number of reasons we lost, including the fact that Hays was a very good team, it presented an opportunity to mediate and receive words that I hoped would put the game behind us as well as teach another life lesson. I should not have been surprised that the team responded above and beyond, as you will see.

> To every [thing there is] a season, and a time to every purpose under the heaven…A time to get, and a time to lose; a time to keep, and a time to cast away
>
> Ecclesiastes 3:1, 6 (KJV)

## No Excuses

The ref's were bad
'Twas their home floor
Two of the reasons
I know there's more.
You came to play
But lost the game.
Whatever the cause
The score stays the same.
Whenever it happens
By luck or design,
Blame no one else
For it may be a sign
To look at yourself
Your effort, your will.
Is *trust* still strong?
How about your skill?
For there's games ahead
And you've been blessed
With another chance

To pass the test.
So make no excuse
But get yourself set
For another run
'Cause you're not done yet!
1/12/2006

# ENJOY THE RIDE

One of the things that I have learned through my coaching experience is that while you wait and wait for the season to start, once it starts, it seems to fly by. Because this team was so special, I wanted to convey to them to make sure to enjoy each moment of their success, because that is where the real joy comes, a play made, a defensive stop. It is moment by moment. History will record wins and losses, championships and records. But the real pleasure is seized from the moments one plays. "Enjoy the Ride" was a reminder to coaches and players alike to take time to savor those moments without the pressure of the final goal.

[As for] man, his days [are] as grass: as a flower of the field, so he flourisheth.

For the wind passeth over it, and it is gone; and the place thereof shall know it no more.

Psalms 103:15–16 (KJV)

# Enjoy the Ride

Highly regarded and highly ranked
Some special wins you've already banked.
But with more to come, bigger games ahead
You must hear these words that need to be said.
Because your season grows shorter each day
Savor each moment of each game you play.
Don't rush to the finish for there's more to learn
Your team to strengthen, new rewards to earn.
Never lose sight of the ultimate prize
Yet mark each success when before you it lies.
Let Trust be your bond with your heart your guide
And no matter what *enjoy the ride!*
1/17/2006

# WILL YOU BE THERE?

Having first considered the moment, it was time to consider the ultimate goal. Almost all of the team had been a part of last season's championship team. I was inspired to remind them of that experience. "Will You be There" in its original form was posted with a picture of the Kansas Expocentre in Topeka, the home of the 5A state championship.

Once again it proved to be prophetic in nature as the team would take it to heart.

> For which of you, intending to build a tower, sitteth not down first, and counteth the cost, whether he have [sufficient] to finish [it]?
>
> Luke 14:28 (KJV)

# Will You Be There?

The time is coming,
It's not far away,
When losers walk,
And Winners stay,
Champions are crowned,
And last games are played,
Trust in your *team*,
Do not be afraid,
For this is the season,
You've seen in your *dreams*,
Let *faith* be the beacon,
From inside you that beams,
No matter the venue,
No matter the foe,
Your remaining games,
Are chances to grow,
Your *heart* will be tested,
Your skills will be tried,
The answers you'll seek,

Must be found deep inside,
Just sacrifice all,
And right now prepare,
Then in that moment,
You know you'll be there.
1/28/2006

# BREAK OUT

"Break Out" was the first in a series of poems I was given to challenge the team down the stretch. Although we were playing well, we seemed to be in a rut or a slump. In the words were both a challenge and a warning. The team, however, would follow their coaches' advice and began to take their game to the next level. They continued to define and accept their roles and prepared for an even bigger finish.

> Wherefore seeing we also are compassed about with so great a cloud of witnesses, let us lay aside every weight, and the sin which doth so easily beset [us], and let us run with patience the race that is set before us.
>
> Hebrews 12:1 (KJV)

## Break Out

You've seen the rankings,
You've heard the cheers.
Beware of the trap
That before you appears.
For peril awaits
A *team* that rests
In the comfort of
Its past success.
Are you as good
As the prophets say?
Are you a *team*
That'll go all the way?
You hold the answers
You hold the key
For there's more to your game
Than we've yet to see.
Demand from yourself
And seek from your *team*
Their total effort

In pursuit of the *dream*.
"No less than my best"
Let this be your vow
Break out right here
Break out right now!
2/9/2006

# PROVE IT

High School Basketball in Kansas is said to have three seasons: before Christmas, after Christmas, and the postseason. The 05–06 GBHS Panthers finished the regular season 19–1. They were ranked number one in 5A. But, in reality, the real season was just beginning. "Prove It" was both a celebration of what they had done and a challenge to leave their mark in history as back-to-back state champions. Did they really posses the heart of a champion? Only time and five more games would tell.

> And be not conformed to this world: but be ye transformed by the renewing of your mind, that ye may prove what [is] that good, and acceptable, and perfect, will of God.
>
> Romans 12:2 (KJV)

# Prove It

Unbeaten at *home*
Nineteen and one
No small achievement
A job well done!
A well-balanced *team*
One of the best
Whose goals were met
As they passed each test.
These are the claims
You now can make
Still they don't compare
To what remains at stake.
Do you *love* enough?
Do you *trust* your *team?*
Are you next in line
To *fulfill* the *dream?*
Don't shout out "Yes"
Or nod your head
Just close your eyes

Think on this instead.
Give all you have
In the days that remain
And push yourself
Beyond the edge of pain.
As by words your fate
Is seldom moved
But by your actions
Your *heart* is proved.
2/26/2006

# RIGHT NOW

With convincing wins over Salina Central and Salina South, GBHS advanced to the state tournament as the number one seed. However first round opponent Emporia was very much a threat. Coaches Wetig and Baker continued their mastery of motivation as they had done all season, following Coach Langrehr's lead. We returned to a theme they knew well and "Right Now" would be my contribution, penned again in the practice gym and posted prior to the game, as had become a tradition. The team responded as we had now come to expect them to, and advanced to the semifinal game.

> Say not ye, There are yet four months, and [then] cometh harvest? behold, I say unto you, Lift up your eyes, and look on the fields; for they are white already to harvest.
>
> John 4:35 (KJV)

# Right Now

Your practice is over
The walk-throughs are done
Now it is time
To get the job done.
It's not for the glory
It's not for the fame
It's all for the *love*
You share for the *game*.
It's all about *trust*
It's all about *team*
Giving all that you have
In pursuit of the *dream*.
You've been here before
You know what to do
The *faith* that's within
Will see you through.
So respect your foes
And to your *heart* be true
As you reap the reward

That a *champion* is due.
For no one is promised
More than this day
Seize all that you can
From each moment you play.
3/8/2006

# RIGHT HERE

The semifinal foe was a very talented McPherson team. GBHS had beaten them on their home floor before the Christmas break and a tough game was anticipated. The second part of last year's motto "Right Here" appeared to fit this game. I hoped they would understand how they arrived here and what a special place it was. They did and advanced to the championship game against Topeka Highland Park.

> Who shall ascend into the hill of the LORD? or who shall stand in his holy place? He that hath clean hands, and a pure heart; who hath not lifted up his soul unto vanity, nor sworn deceitfully. He shall receive the blessing from the LORD, and righteousness from the God of his salvation.
>
> Psalms 24:3–5 (KJV)

## Right Here

With each shot you have taken
Every game you have played
A course has been charted
Your path has been made.
With the *dream* as your guide
You have come to this place
Let *trust* rule your thoughts
As this challenge you face.
The strength you have gained
Will be tested today
Your *heart* will be proved
By the way that you play.
For this game's the next stop
On your quest for the prize
Makes the most of this chance
Which before you now lies.
3/10/2006

# THE CHAMPIONSHIP GAME

Although we were the number one seed, we found that we were once again an underdog in some people's eyes as Highland Park was a very talented team and boasted that they had not lost to another 5A team all year. As in the preceding year, Coach Langrehr determined to play our game. Another one of his philosophies also came to the fore—"Respect everyone, Fear no one." "The Championship Game" was intended to convey the importance of maintaining your team identity, and doing the things that brought you to that point, without concern over what would happen in the end. They did not disappoint themselves or their many fans who were on hand to celebrate GBHS's second state championship as they went "back to back."

And every man that striveth for the mastery is
temperate in all things. Now they [do it] to obtain
a corruptible crown; but we an incorruptible. I
therefore so run, not as uncertainly; so fight I, not
as one that beateth the air

I Corinthians 9:25–26 (KJV)

# The Championship Game

It's the end of the season
One game left to play
"What a wonderful ride!"
Is all I can say.
In the game that remains
You must answer the call,
Stand together as one
Fear nothing at all.
*Trust* all that you know
*Trust* what you will do
*Trust* all your teammates
*Trust* will see you through.
Know in your *heart*
This is where you belong
You'll forever stand tall
If you finish strong.
3/11/2006

# THANKS

"Thanks" really doesn't need much of an explanation, but I will give it anyway. This team finished with a school best record of 24–1 and a second state championship. They showed great character and were an excellent example of a true team. Their hard work and all of the lessons they learned proved the heart they had. I am thankful that I was able to be a part of it all. On a personal level, I wanted to show my thanks to be on the bench and in the locker room with Jon and to be a part of his success. Many coaches with far greater credentials than mine have never received the opportunity to do what I have done. I pray that I never forget this blessing and hope that I have at least in some small part given back some of what I have received.

That I may publish with the voice of thanksgiving, and tell of all thy wondrous works.

Psalms 26:7 (KJV)

## Thanks

I'll try to express
With words that will rhyme
How proud I am
Of you at this time.
In pursuit of the *dream*
What we have shared
To the wealth of a king
Can not be compared.
By the *trust* you have earned,
The *love* that you've shown
The *heart* you have proved
You'll forever be known.
For those who will follow
And those who still play
I honor you now
For marking the way.
Know I have been blessed
By each moment you played
For what's been invested
I've been more than repaid.
3/14/2006

# DREAM FULFILLED II

"Dream Fulfilled II" was also a must, as I wanted the players of this team to see their victories in the context of life. Everything that they had learned in the course of the season and the games they played should carry them far in life if they apply those very same principles. My dream will be to watch them grow as players, then men, husbands, and fathers of children with their own dreams.

> Wherefore the rather, brethren, give diligence to make your calling and election sure: for if ye do these things, ye shall never fall.
>
> II Peter 1:10 (KJV)

## Dream Fulfilled II:
### *(The Eternal Dream)*

You've tasted the best
That the *game* has to give
But it's only the start
Of the life you must live.
With the talent you have
And all you have learned
There shall come a time
When it must be returned.
As you played with your *team*
Your spirit was freed
Now it rises within
It will help you succeed.
So wherever you go
Follow your *heart*
Be worthy of *trust*
Know always your part.
Remember whenever
A goal has been met
To look up and know

That you're not done yet!
For this *dream* is eternal
A part of *his* plan
Live your life as a player
And not as a fan.
3/15/2006

# COMMENCEMENT

With the end of Jon's senior year, I had hoped to receive the inspiration to write something profound to wrap up his high school career. I don't know how profound "Commencement" proved to be, but it certainly helped me put in perspective that he had completed high school and how fast it seemed to have gone. Jon (without any input from me) gave an outstanding speech at commencement, proving once again that the son had eclipsed the father, and I was very proud of him. I still think "Commencement" reflects the heart of every parent at graduation, so I have included it in this book.

> He hath shewed thee, O man, what [is] good; and what doth the LORD require of thee, but to do justly, and to love mercy, and to walk humbly with thy God?
>
> Micah 6:8 (KJV)

# Commencement

So long ago
When you had your first day
This moment in time
Seemed so far away.
Each day was special
It seems now a blur
I see you now
And think how you were.
Still it's time to reflect
On what you have learned
The tests you have faced,
The rewards you have earned.
Not of the kind
You win through a *game*
Hang 'round your neck,
Or will bring you fame.
They're etched on your *heart*
They're stored in your mind,
Found in your *dreams*

And the skills you've refined.
The courage to rise
Beyond and above
The power of *trust*
The strength of *love.*
For all this and more
Give thanks today
For all who have taught
And shown you the way.
As you walk across,
As you shake their hands
Accept the challenge
Which before you now stands.
A new stage appears
As this curtain falls
Embrace your role
For destiny calls.
5/7/2006

# CARRY THE TORCH

With Jon and the other seniors graduated, it was time to look to the future. We had another group of returning players, all who had patiently waited for their turn. I was reminded of one of Coach Langrehr's suggestion for a theme that "Tradition never Graduates," which when coupled with the importance of "Trust" to our program led to the summer camp poem of "Carry the Torch."

> Ye are the light of the world. A city that is set on an hill cannot be hid. Neither do men light a candle, and put it under a bushel, but on a candlestick; and it giveth light unto all that are in the house. Let your light so shine before men, that they may see your good works, and glorify your Father which is in heaven.
>
> Matthew 5:14–16 (KJV)

## Carry the Torch

To some it seems worn
For some it feels new,
Still the torch of *trust*
Has been passed to you.
*Trust* in your skill
*Trust* in your *team*
*Trust* in your *heart*
*Trust* in the *dream*.
Carry it high
As now you prepare
The symbol of
The bonds you share.
Your strength of spirit
Your *love* for the *game,*
Your will to succeed
Are ever the same.
For the *call* you hear,
The games you will play,
'though they seem far off
Grow closer each day.
6/8/2006

# ONE HEARTBEAT

Before I reached the next basketball season, I received another message from Coach Bo Black. Since he has been in Great Bend, he has used a "Band of Brothers" motto and in the fall of 2006. The take on it was "One Heartbeat." As you have seen from past poems, heart is essential to our success, so I was given again to take his lead, and "One Heartbeat" was the result. Although this team lost a hard-fought 5A state championship game, they carried GBHS football tradition to new heights and demonstrated how a team with a single mind and heart could transcend individual ability.

> Two [are] better than one; because they have a good reward for their labour. For if they fall, the one will lift up his fellow: but woe to him [that is] alone when he falleth; for [he hath] not another to help him up.
>
> Ecclesiastes 4:9–10 (KJV)

# One Heartbeat

In every *heart*
There lives a *dream.*
For every player
There is a *team*
Banded as one
Through *love* for the *game.*
The power of *trust,*
The drive to claim
Rewards they are due,
Life's lessons to learn,
Honor to show,
And honor to earn.
Joined forever
By a single beat
Over and over
May it ever repeat.
7/2/2006

# THE NEXT LEVEL

There were changes at the Pike household in the fall of 2006. First, Jon accepted the opportunity to continue playing basketball for Coach Fletchall at Barton County Community College. Second, Jeff was starting 8th grade, which in Great Bend is the first time for interscholastic competition. "The Next Level" was written for both of them as they faced new challenges and different levels of competition.

> But they that wait upon the LORD shall renew [their] strength; they shall mount up with wings as eagles; they shall run, and not be weary; [and] they shall walk, and not faint.
>
> Isaiah 40:31 (KJV)

## The Next Level

The sun has risen
On a brand new day
As you've been blessed
With new games to play.
What brought you this far
You must never forget
A champion's *heart*
The hard work and sweat.
The power of *trust*
The thrill of the chase
The strength of the *team*
When each knows his place.
Your *love* for the *game*
Will be tested each day
Let it reflect
In each moment you play.
May your *faith* be strong
And your spirit revel
While you take your game
To a higher level.
8/22/2006

# FULFILL THE DREAM III

As basketball season approached, I was excited because as a parent and spectator, I had plenty to watch, but with no one in high school, I would be able to concentrate completely on coaching without balancing the coach/father act. I could not resist the temptation of "Fulfill the Dream III," and continued with the tradition theme. Looking back, I can see that this team fully accepted their responsibility to continue the tradition and gave tremendous effort in pursuit of their own dream.

> [Let] nothing [be done] through strife or vainglory; but in lowliness of mind let each esteem other better than themselves. Look not every man on his own things, but every man also on the things of others.
>
> Philippians 2:3–4 (KJV)

# Fulfill the Dream III:
### *(Tradition Remains)*

From the beginning
These traits you share
As for their cause
You sweat and prepare.
*Love* for the *game*
*Faith* in your *team*
The strength of *heart*
To pursue the *dream.*
Well you have learned
The value of *trust*
Use all your skill
To do what you must.
'Though faces will change
And the tests are new
Tradition remains
For it resides in you!
9/21/2006

# WILL IT BE YOU?

In keeping with past years, before we started playing, I wanted to challenge our players to see themselves as they would like to be—champions. I also wanted them to remind themselves of what they had experienced and seen. "Will it be You?" took a different form than other poems I have been given. I wonder if it isn't because it is a question we all should ask ourselves every day as long as we are on this earth.

> And whatsoever ye do, do [it] heartily, as to the LORD, and not unto men; Knowing that of the LORD ye shall receive the reward of the inheritance: for ye serve the LORD Christ.
>
> Colossians 3:23–24 (KJV)

## Will it Be You?

The call of the *game*
Goes forth anew
Someone must answer,
Will it be you?

A champion's *heart*
Beats in but a few
Strength for the test
Does it beat in you?

*Love* is the soul
And *trust* the glue
The *team* requires
Are they found in you?

A price there is
For a *dream* come true
It demands your best
Will it be paid by you?

The victor captures
The reward he is due
No room for doubt
Will it be you?

The tradition stands
Who will see it through?
Accept the challenge?
*Will it be you?*
11/11/2006

# NOW IS THE TIME

"Now is the Time" came to me as I was driving back from Colby where I had gone to watch Jon and Barton play. Being in the building where I used to practice and play some twenty-nine years ago, and then seeing Jon on the same court, caused a lot of different thoughts to swirl around in my mind. But once again, His voice cut through all of the different thoughts to remind me that it had all been for a purpose, and that purpose was the here and now, not the world of what was or what might have been. It was a reality check for me and I shared it with the team in the hope that it would give them reassurance that if they kept what they knew, they would navigate the uncertainty ahead. With or without this inspiration, they continued through the regular season, undefeated at home with an 18–2 mark, and an undisputed WAC championship.

Take therefore no thought for the morrow: for the morrow shall take thought for the things of itself. Sufficient unto the day [is] the evil thereof.

Matthew 6:34 (KJV)

## Now Is the Time

Another game
A long trip home
The mind, it wanders
My thoughts, they roam.
From whence we came,
Where we are now,
Where we are going,
Will we get there somehow?
New goals to achieve
With each passing day
Dreams to fulfill
With each game we play.
What are the answers?
Wherein lies the key?
Then the voice inside
Speaks clearly to me:
It burns in the *heart*,
Fueled by the *dream*
Forged with *trust*,

And the *love* of the *team*.
So ponder not
What's held in store
*Now* is the time
To be accounted for.
1/27/2007

# WHO ARE YOU?

As we prepared for sub-state, I was again led to ask this team to remember who they were. Every team is different in composition, and this group was more free-spirited, yet still banded by the common dream. "Who are You" was a reminder to us all that we do not live in a vacuum and many people and events shape who we are. It was also a call to consider who they were and their ability to rise to whatever challenge may lie before them.

> And we **know** that all things work together for good to them that love God, to them **who** are the called according to [his] purpose.
>
> Romans 8:28 (KJV)

# Who Are You?

The end approaches,
The bracket is set
The gauntlet thrown,
A goal must be met.
Take time now,
Before you play,
To consider how
You've arrived at this day.
Given a *heart*,
And a body that's strong,
Skills you have learned
And honed all along.
Family whose labors,
Efforts and sweat
Are rewarded now,
You must never forget.
Coaches who taught,
Planned and prepared,
All for the *love* of the *game* that is shared.

Teammates of old,
And those you now *trust,*
To share the load,
Do what they must.
All this and more
Shaped who you are,
Carried you on,
Brought you this far.
Let your passion burn,
Your spirit rise,
For you were created
To compete for the prize.
2/27/2007

# MAKE YOUR MARK

Almost all of the 06–07 team had been a part of the prior championship team. They were determined to three-peat. No one would argue that we were a much different team. Likewise, I don't think that anyone would argue that this team played as hard and gave as much effort as anyone could ask for. If they were to win, it would have to be their own way. "Make Your Mark" was written and posted before the sub-state championship game, again against archrival Hays. As they had done all year, the Panthers came out and did it their way, advancing to state for the third straight year.

> And whatsoever ye do in word or deed, [do] all in the name of the LORD Jesus, giving thanks to God and the Father by him.
>
> Colossians 3:17

## Make Your Mark

So many times
You've taken the floor.
Now it is time
To take it once more.
But this will be one
You'll always keep
In your mind, your *heart*,
Your *dreams* as you sleep.
'Though you've been a part
Of the *teams* of the past,
This is your turn
The die has been cast.
It's not about who
It's all about HOW
So make your mark
*Right here and right now!*
*3/30/2007*

# A DREAM (TO BE) FULFILLED

The Panther's first round opponent was Wichita-Kapaun, a team we had beaten earlier at the El Dorado tournament. Due to my schedule, I was unable to go up with the team as I had done in the past, and arrived shortly before game time, something I now regret. No new poems and we dusted off the ones from the past. Sadly, cold shooting and foul trouble brought an early end to our run for a third championship. As we prepared for our traditional dinner, I was reminded of what started this all, "For the Love of the Game," and that the true "Dream" is the pursuit of any dream, and I will always be proud to have been a part of this team as well. Again, in life, we do not win every game and "A Dream (to be) Fulfilled" is a message for life as well as for a season.

> I therefore, the prisoner of the LORD, beseech you that ye walk worthy of the vocation wherewith ye are called.
>
> Ephesians 4:1 (KJV)

# A Dream (to Be) Fulfilled

Your season ended just short of your *dream*
But there's no shame for you and the *team*.

Your record will stand as one of the best
Your *heart* was proved as you faced each test.

You made your mark. The standard you raised
For this and more you'll always be praised.

Through strength you found in *love* for the *game*
By *trust* you earned you'll not be the same.

New seasons approach, a lifetime as well
You are prepared to answer the bell.

It's never who It is always *how*
Not tomorrow Right *here* and right *now*.

For you I pray a purpose, a theme
A life fulfilled the ultimate *dream.*
3/31/2007

# IT'S NOT ENOUGH

I thought I was done for the year, but when Coach Langrehr's baseball team qualified for state in the spring, I was compelled to write one more. There is always a temptation to relax when you reach a certain place you have searched for, and I desired to encourage them to finish what they started. Again, it was not meant to be as their season ended in the first round with what was still a very good 20–3 record. For all of us, just getting there should not be enough and we should continue to seek our best.

> Boast not thyself of to morrow; for thou knowest not what a day may bring forth.
>
> Proverbs 27:1 (KJV)

# It's Not Enough

You won and advanced your *dream* still lives,
A shot at the title and the best the *game* gives.

Enjoy the moment then set your *heart*
Hold nothing back prepare from the start.

Though it's quite the feat
And it's always tough
Just getting there
Can't be enough.
5/18/2007

# THE PRAYER TRILOGY

The coaches', athletes', and parents' prayers were written as I meditated on what I wished I was, had been, and could still be. Many different coaches, players, and parents, including my own, have inspired these thoughts. I would be lying if I were to say I've always been true to the thoughts expressed therein, but that is the nature of a prayer and I hope to one day attain such a position and place.

> …The effectual fervent prayer of a righteous man availeth much.
>
> James 5:16 (KJV)

> Train up a child in the way he should go: and when he is old, he will not depart from it.
>
> Proverbs 22:6 (KJV)

The LORD [is] nigh unto all them that call upon
him, to all that call upon him in truth. He will fulfill
the desire of them that fear him: he also will hear
their cry, and will save them.

Psalms145:18–19 (KJV)

I have fought a good fight, I have finished [my]
course, I have kept the faith.

II Timothy 4:7 (KJV)

# The Coach's Prayer

I come to you Lord as I start my day
And for your wisdom I humbly pray.
Thank you for the chances to teach
Through this game I love, my players to reach.
Your enduring love let me strive to show
So you and each other they will come to know.
Walk with me and run with my team,
Give me the vision, give them the dream.
If today we practice, plan and prepare,
May I give the most in the time we share.
If we're ahead at the end of the day
I will give the credit to those who did play,
The rest of the team, our supporters and fans
Before I accept any praise for my plans.
If time runs out before our comeback is done,
Let me take the blame, the gauntlet run.
Inside of each one let me see what can be
May I never expect more of them then of me.
When its time to correct may I always be fair,

To earn respect, create a bond to share.
Bless my family for the sacrifice they make
Their support for granted may I never take.
And if I should miss a sign or your call
Forgive me and, pick me up if I fall.
11/1/2004

# The Athlete's Prayer

Teach me O Lord to walk in your way,
So your will I may do thru this sport that I play.
Let me honor you first, then my parents and team,
And the words of my coaches may I always esteem.
As you laid down your life, a ransom for men,
Let me sacrifice self, so the team may win.
I will always give thanks for the chance to compete,
In the joy of a win, in the pain of defeat.
May I ever keep the trust of my friends,
For its worth isn't measured by losses or wins.
Whatever my duty, whatever my role,
Help me give my all for the common goal.
So when the last horn sounds, and I walk away,
I'll have no regrets, and with Paul I can say,
"I have run the race that was before me laid,
And your glory I've seen in each game that I've
played."
9/10/2005

# The Parent's Prayer

Thank you Lord for this child of mine
For the games he plays are by your design.
I remember when he first learned to run
And will never forget when he played just for fun.
But years have passed and time has flown,
The seeds that were planted are now full grown.
So in how I act, in what I say,
May I never forget it's his turn to play.
I will look not for glory in honors earned,
And instead take pride in the lessons he's learned.
For headlines will fade and medals will rust,
They cannot compare to the value of *trust*.
To plan and prepare, yes, even *dream*
Have all been taught as part of the *team*.
Giving his all for the sake of his friends,
Is another theme that never ends.
These lessons of life and so much more
Flow from the *game* no matter the score.
Show him your will, and come what may,

Your hand from his shoulder do not take away.
May his love for the *game* never grow stale,
Let him know in his heart your love will not fail.
Into your hands his *team* I place,
Protect them on each mission they face.
Forget not his coaches with their part in your plans,
Their rewards should be greater than parents' and fans.'
And for this moment, this hour, this day,
I thank you again and humbly pray,
In all that I do, in all that I dare,
Help me make the most of this time we share.
10/28/2005

# CONCLUSION

It's taken some time to commit these thoughts, concerning the poems, to writing. Most, if not all, are personal reflections on what I have seen and felt. One never knows what tomorrow holds, but I am thankful for the experiences and people the game has brought into my life. I don't know when my season as coach will be over, but Jeff is starting high school, so the adventure continues. Coach Jim Valvano once said, "Other people go to an office. I get to coach. I know I've been blessed." If so, I am doubly blessed as I get to do both. As long as He will allow it, I intend to pursue this dream.

Chuck Pike